2490

Wildfire Alert!

Lynn Peppas

Crabtree Publishing Company
www.crabtreebooks.com

Crabtree Publishing Company

www.crabtreebooks.com

PMB 16A, 350 Fifth Avenue
Suite 3308
New York, NY 10118

612 Welland Avenue,
St. Catharines
Ontario, Canada
L2M 5V6

73 Lime Walk
Headington
Oxford 0X3 7AD
United Kingdom

In memory of my mother, Doreen Ellis MacIntyre, who taught me to love books.

Coordinating editor: Ellen Rodger

Project editor: Carrie Gleason

Copy editor: Sean Charlebois

Proofreader: Adrianna Morganelli

Designer and production coordinator: Rosie Gowsell

Art director: Rob MacGregor

Photo research: Allison Napier

Indexer: Wendy Scavuzzo

Prepress: Embassy Graphics

Printing: Worzalla Publishing Company

Consultant: Dr. Richard Cheel, Professor of Earth Sciences, Brock University

Photographs: ADAMS/HANSEN PHOTOGRAPHY: p. 12 (bottom); AFP/CORBIS/MAGMA: p. 20 (middle); Brent Bear: p. 8 (bottom); Bettmann/CORBIS/MAGMA: p. 18 (bottom); Jonathan Blair/ CORBIS/MAGMA: p. 16; Tom Brownold: p. 10 (bottom); Lloyd Cluff /CORBIS/MAGMA: p. 18 (middle); CORBIS/MAGMA: p. 23 (bottom); Rick D'Elia/CORBIS/MAGMA: p. 24 (bottom); Araldo de Luca/CORBIS/MAGMA: p. 5 (bottom); Yves Forestier/ CORBIS SYGMA/MAGMA: p. 26 (bottom); Raymond Gehman/CORBIS/ MAGMA: p. 10 (bottom), p. 29 (bottom); Gibson Stock Photo: p. 5 (top), p. 20 (top); Bob Grabowski: p. 11 (top); Richard Hamilton Smith/CORBIS/MAGMA: p. 13 (top); Jeff Henry/Roche Jaune Pictures Inc: p. 12 (bottom), p. 22 (bottom); Historical Picture Archive/ CORBIS/MAGMA: p. 19 (bottom); Jeremy Horner/ CORBIS/ MAGMA: p. 11 (bottom); Sam Kleinman/CORBIS/ MAGMA: p. 5 (top, right);

Lawrence Manning/ CORBIS/MAGMA: p. 22 (top); William Manning/CORBIS/MAGMA: p. 8 (top, inset); BillMARCHEL.com: title page; William Munoz: p. 13 (middle); Gunter Marx Photography /CORBIS/MAGMA: p. 27 (top); Lucy Nicholson/Reuter Newmedia Inc./CORBIS/MAGMA: cover; Richard Nowitz/ CORBIS/MAGMA: p. 21 (bottom); Douglas Peebles/CORBIS/ MAGMA: p. 9 (top, inset); JIM REED/SCIENCE PHOTO LIBRARY: p. 11 (right); Reuters Newmedia Inc./CORBIS/ MAGMA: p. 17 (top); Lynda Richardson/CORBIS/ MAGMA: p. 29 (top); Paul M. Ross Jr/911 pictures: p. 7 (bottom), p. 25 (top); Galen Rowell/CORBIS/MAGMA: p. 27; Royalty-Free/CORBIS/ MAGMA: p. 20 (bottom), p. 23 (top); Joel Sartore/CORBIS/MAGMA: p. 7 (middle); Phil Schermeister/ CORBIS/MAGMA: p. 7 (top); Dean Sewell: p. 4 (both), p. 17 (bottom); Pascale Treichler/Getty Images: p. 3; J. Vasconcelos/Ambient Images: p. 21 (top); Airphoto- Jim Wark: p. 15 (top); Karen Wattenmaker/911 Pictures: p. 25, p. 26 (top), p. 28 (bottom)

Illustrations: Robert MacGregor: p. 6, p. 9 (bottom), p. 15 (bottom); David Wysotski, Allure Illustrations: pp. 30-31

Cover: Firefighters fighting wildfires in Simi Valley, California, October 29, 2003.

Contents: The branches on this tree are glowing embers from a fire.

Title page: Fire whirls are large columns of fire that can develop during a wildfire.

Published by
Crabtree Publishing Company

Copyright © 2004

Cataloging-in-Publication Data

Peppas, Lynn.
    Wildfire alert! / Lynn Peppas.
        p. cm. -- (Disaster alert!)
        ISBN 0-7787-1574-4 (rlb) -- ISBN 0-7787-1606-6 (pbk.)
    1. Wildfires--Juvenile literature. 2. Forest fires--Juvenile literature.
I. Title. II. Series.
    SD421.23.P46 2004
    363.37'9--dc22
                                                    2004000882
                                                    LC

Table of Contents

Fire's Two Faces

Fire can be nature's best friend or most destructive enemy. At one time people depended on fire to cook their food and heat their homes, but fire could just as easily destroy homes and take the lives of people and animals. When under control, fire is beneficial, but when it gets out of hand, it becomes a wildfire, and its destruction is devastating.

(right) Newscasts often only show fire as a danger or a threat, such as forcing this family to flee an Australian forest fire, or bushfire.

What is a disaster? A disaster is a destructive event that affects the natural world and human communities. Some disasters are predictable and others occur without warning. Coping successfully with a disaster depends on a community's preparation.

(left) House fires put people in danger. Unfortunately, people are also the main cause of the fires.

(right) The Olympic torch is a positive fire symbol around the world.

From the ashes

The phoenix was an ancient Egyptian legend. The bird had beautiful golden-red feathers that looked like flames. There was only one phoenix, which lived for 500 years. Before the phoenix's death, it built a nest, which burst into flame, killing the phoenix. From the ashes, a new phoenix was born. This legend shows what the ancient Egyptians thought about the destructive nature of fire, but also the promise of new life from its ashes.

What is fire?

Fire needs three ingredients to burn: oxygen, fuel, and heat. This is called the fire triangle. If one of the ingredients is missing, a fire will not start. If one is taken away, a fire will extinguish.

Fuel

Fuels are materials that feed a fire. In the forest, grasses, shrubs, trees, leaves, and plants are fuels. Dry or dead fuels burn more easily than fuels that are wet, or alive. Live plants do not catch fire easily because they contain water, which cools the heat and does not allow oxygen to reach the fuel's surface.

Oxygen

Oxygen is a gas found in the atmosphere. A fire takes oxygen from the surrounding air.

Oxygen

Fuel

Heat

Heat

When oxygen mixes with fuel, a change, or chemical reaction, called oxidization occurs. When heat is added to oxygen and fuel, a fast and violent type of oxidization happens and the fuel begins burning. This burning is called combustion.

Pre-heating

For a fire to start, fuel must be heated. This is called pre-heating. All fuels have different temperatures at which they burn, called an ignition, or flash, point. Wood's ignition point is 800 degrees Fahrenheit (427 degrees Celsius). The heat created by a fire preheats the surrounding fuel, so it too will easily catch fire.

(right) Radiant heat is heat energy that comes in waves, or rays, from the source to the fuel. The heat from a campfire is radiant heat.

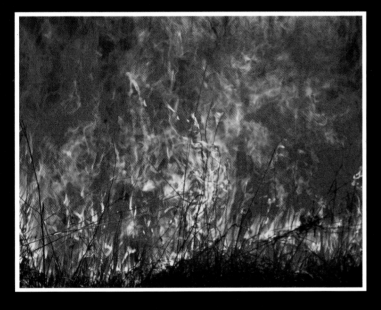

Flaming combustion

The second stage of a fire is called flaming combustion. When a fuel reaches its ignition point, it begins to break down into **flammable** gases, tars, charcoal, water, and ash. The flammable gases rise up to the surface of the fuel and react with oxygen in the air. Flame is the result of a gas reacting to the oxygen surrounding it.

(left) Flaming combustion is the stage of fire we most recognize.

Glowing combustion

Glowing combustion is the final stage of a fire. During this stage the fuel itself burns. Embers, or the remains of fuel, can burn for days or even weeks after a fire has swept through an area.

(right) The fire goes out when there is no more fuel to burn, oxygen supply is cut off, or the heat source is cooled.

Forests and Fires

A forest is a natural balance of living plants and animals called an ecosystem. Fire is a part of this ecosystem. Fires clean the dead fuel littering the forest floor, giving some species of plants room to grow.

Boreal forests

Boreal forests are a type of forest located across the northern regions of North America, Europe, and Asia. Winters are cold and long, and summers are short and warm in these forests. Coniferous trees that have needles and cones, called evergreens, grow here. Needles are a type of leaf that are wax-covered and very thin, and do not dry up and fall off seasonally. Fires are not common in boreal forests, but when they do happen, they are large and **intense**.

(above) Almost all trees in boreal forests are coniferous, which means they stay green all year round. For this reason, the trees are also called evergreens.

Temperate forests

Temperate forests have changing seasons with warm summers and cool winters. These forests are located in milder areas such as central North America, Europe, and China. Temperate forests get **precipitation** year-round, although southern areas have dry spells during summer. These forests are home to deciduous trees with broadleaves. The leaves change color in autumn, fall off during winter, and grow back in spring. The dead leaves form debris on the forest floor, which decays quickly leaving little fuel for forest fires. Hot, dry summers with lightning storms regularly start fires in these forests. The fires are usually not intense because they lack debris to fuel them.

(below) Most of the trees in temperate forests are deciduous, which includes maple and oak trees. The leaves of these trees change color in autumn.

Tropical rainforests

Tropical rainforests are located around the equator. These forests do not have seasons and are moist and warm all the time. Tropical forests have more plants and tree life than any other forests because of their climate. Rainforests do not have debris on their forest floor because when a tree dies, or leaves fall to the ground, insects called termites break it down very fast. Wildfires rarely occur in tropical rainforests.

The forest floor of a rainforest is damp, dark, and warm. The plants that grow there do not easily catch fire because their leaves contain so much moisture.

Photosynthesis

Forests are areas of tree and plant life that create the oxygen that animals and humans breathe. Through a process called photosynthesis, green leaves convert the sun's energy into food using a substance called chlorophyll. Carbon dioxide from the air enters leaves through small holes called stomata where it combines with the stored energy through a chemical reaction to make food. Oxygen is released in the process.

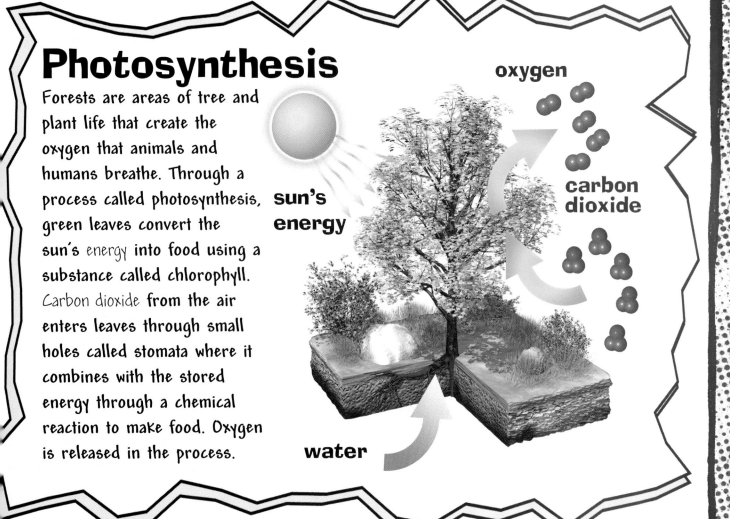

oxygen

carbon dioxide

sun's energy

water

Prescribed fires

At one time, forest firefighters put out all fires. Scientists and forest rangers began to notice that some forests began to change. Fires are part of the natural growth cycle of forests. When fires do not burn, the forest **canopy** prevents sunlight from reaching the forest floor, and plants cannot grow. The forest floor also accumulates a dangerous amount of debris. When fires in the forests are **suppressed**, small shrubs and bushes overcrowd the forest floor and there is no room for tree **saplings** to grow. When a wildfire does occur, it becomes large and unmanageable.

Prescribed fires are closely watched fires purposely started by firefighters in an effort to prevent an uncontrollable wildfire. Forest rangers and firefighters start prescribed fires when the weather is humid, cool, and the winds are calm to prevent it from spreading.

(above) This firefighter is starting a prescribed fire to rid the forest floor of fuel.

(below) Sequoias are the largest trees on Earth. At one time, sequoia saplings on North America's Pacific coast could not take root on the forest floor because of all the debris left from suppressed fires.

Ash and nutrients

Forest fires leave ash on the forest floor. Ash is a nutrient, or food, for new plants. When **organic fuel,** such as wood, burns, it breaks down into water, smoke, carbon, and ash. Ash is the non-burnable part of wood. Ashes rise up in smoke, and eventually settles back to the ground. After a fire, **minerals** in ash **fertilize** the soil.

(left) About five years after a fire burned through this national park, new trees have taken root.

Slash and burn

Slash and burn is a method of clearing rainforests for farmland. At the beginning of a dry season, the bark of trees are slashed, stopping the flow of water and nutrients into the tree and killing it. The tree branches are then cut off and put at the bottom of the trunk in a circle. A fire is started to burn and clear the trees and vegetation. The ash from the burned trees fertilizes the soil for growing crops. In slash and burn agriculture, the soil is only good for a few years, until the nutrients are used up. New areas are cleared, and more rainforest is killed.

Types of Wildfire

A wildfire is an uncontrolled fire that spreads very quickly. There are three types of forest fires that are named after the area of fuel they burn: ground fires, surface fires, and crown fires.

Starting fires

Most wildfires are started by people not properly extinguishing campfires or leaving leaves to burn unsupervised. Other wildfires are caused by lightning. A lightning bolt is only 1/2 inch (1.25 cm) wide, but reaches temperatures of 54,000° Fahrenheit (30,000° Celsius). If a lightning bolt strikes dry fuel, such as a rotten tree, it starts a fire.

Despite warnings and public programs, people are still responsible for most fires.

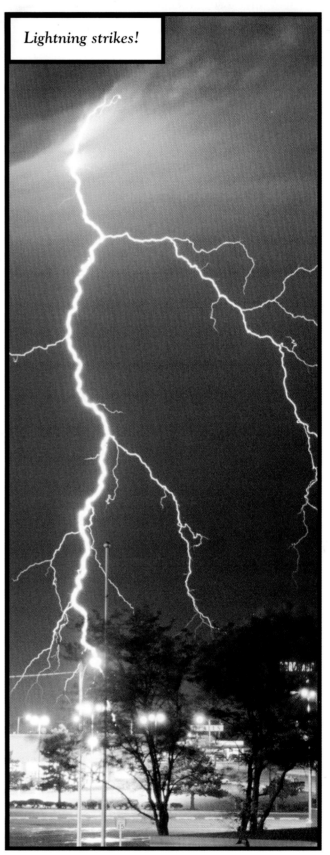

Lightning strikes!

Ground fires

Ground fires are easy to ignite because most fuel on the ground has been dead and decaying for a while. Ground fuels are dry leaves, half-buried pieces of dead wood, and exposed tree roots. Ground fires burn slowly because there is not a lot of oxygen to feed the fire. The flames creep along the bottom of the forest floor and produce a lot of smoke but not many flames. Ground fires are either the beginning of a surface fire, or the end result of a surface or crown fire that has swept through an area.

Surface fires

Surface fires burn the debris and plant life on the forest floor but often do little damage to larger trees in the area. Surface fuels include grasses, shrubs, and fallen branches and trees. There is more oxygen surrounding surface than ground fuels, and as a result, surface fires burn faster and produce more flame. If there is a lot of surface fuel to burn, the fire produces more heat and taller flames. The flames quickly climb dry branches and smaller trees while moving upward into a crown fire.

Crown fires

Crown fires are the most dangerous types of fire because they feed on oxygen from the wind and are very unpredictable. Crown fuels are trees or shrubs that are higher than 4 feet (1.2 meters). The tops of trees burn in crown fires and can quickly be spread by wind.

Ground fire

Surface fire

Crown fire

Fiery Weather

Hot temperatures, little moisture in the air, and strong, gusting winds are the conditions that start a fire and keep it burning.

Fire and water

Low **humidity** and little precipitation mean the fuels that feed fires are dry and easy to spark. Precipitation in the form of rain or snow provides a coating between the fuel and oxygen in the air. This means the chemical reaction between oxygen and fuel necessary for a fire to start cannot take place. If a fire is burning and only a light rain falls, the heat from the fire **evaporates** the rain, which turns to steam before ever reaching the fire.

Fire and wind

Winds push a fire along faster, and help dry out fuels. Large crown fires are so powerful they make their own windy weather called a **firestorm**. Firestorms burn a large amount of fuel quickly and need a lot of oxygen to keep going. When air is heated, it quickly rises up, and cooler air rushes in to replace it. This process is called convection, and the winds the fire sucks in are called convective winds. These strong winds make firestorms dangerously unpredictable, and the toughest type of fire for firefighters to battle.

Spotting

High winds and crown fires can lead to spot fires. Spot fires happen when hot embers from crown fires are carried by the wind to trees further away.

Spot fires can spread fire over rivers.

(above) Fire uses oxygen in the air, leaving very little oxygen for animals or humans to breathe. Burning wood produces a gas which poisons people.

Fire and smoke

Smoke from a fire is deadly to humans and animals. Smoke forms when a **volatile** fuel, such as wood, is heated to about 500° Fahrenheit (260° Celsius). At this temperature, a chemical reaction turns substances in wood from a solid into a gas. This gas is smoke. When the temperature of the wood rises to 800° Fahrenheit (427° Celsius) it ignites, and no more smoke is produced. Instead, the flaming wood produces an invisible gas called carbon monoxide.

A fire whirl is similar to a tornado, which is a violent swirling column of air. When warm air rises, cool air rushes in. As the air quickly rises, it pulls the flames up into a tall column.

15

Famous Forest Fires

Wildfires destroy millions of acres of forest every year. Wildfires become disastrous when they become too large and firefighters can not put them out, and when human lives and homes in their path are at risk.

Yellowstone National Park, U.S.A.

Yellowstone National Park is the first and oldest national park in the world. It has over two million acres of land that sits between three states: Idaho, Montana, and Wyoming. In 1988, a severe **drought** hit the area. On May 24, lightning from a thunderstorm set off the first wildfire of the season. By the beginning of July, fourteen separate fires were raging through the park. Controlled by firefighters, these were allowed to burn. By July 21, the fires covered over 17,000 acres, and over 9,000 firefighters had to be brought in to extinguish the wildfires.

Over 1.4 million acres (566,580 hectares) of the forest, more than half of Yellowstone National Park, burned in the summer of 1988. A snowfall finally ended the fires in November.

Yellowstone National Park, 1988

British Columbia, 2003

By September 2003, over 30,000 people in British Columbia had been evacuated from their homes. In the end, over 300 homes were destroyed by the fires.

British Columbia, Canada

During the summer of 2003, the people of the province of British Columbia, Canada, were fighting severe wildfires due to drought. It was the worst fire season in the province since 1929. The province declared a state of emergency and the Canadian army was brought in to help deal with the effects of the fire. Altogether, over 3,500 firefighters, both professional and volunteer, fought the fires.

Areas of Australia have hot, dry summers, making forest fires common. The wildfires become a problem when they come too close to homes.

Australia

Great City Fires

Some urban fires start as wildfires that move into cities. Other fires in cities are started by human carelessness or by industrial explosions.

Oakland, California fire

The Oakland, California, fire in 1991 started as a forest fire that spread into an urban area. Warm weather and low humidity combined with almost five years of drought-like conditions in the state. Eucalyptus trees imported from Australia supplied a highly flammable fuel because of the oil in their leaves. The fire was pushed by strong winds toward urban areas. Houses, many built with cedar shingles, soon became fuel for the fire. When the fire was finally put out, over 3,000 homes were destroyed and 25 people had died.

California, 1991

Chicago fire

A drought in Chicago, Illinois, in 1871, created the conditions for a massive urban fire. At the time, many of Chicago's buildings were made of wood, as were the streets and sidewalks. The city burned for three days, destroying the city's waterworks and leaving firefighters with no water to fight the fire. A rainfall finally extinguished the fire, but by that time, over 300 people had died and one third of the city was destroyed.

Chicago, Illinois, 1871

Fire of London

In London, England, in the 1600s, there was no public water supply or water pipes to put out a fire. Houses were made of wood, with thatched roofs made of straw or rushes, which were flammable materials. Houses were also built very close together and when one building was on fire it could easily spread to the next. When a fire broke out in a London baker's oven in 1660, everyone left their jobs and formed a bucket brigade to pass water from person to person and extinguish the blaze. Londoners tried this for a little while but the fire grew out of control. The fire burned for five days and destroyed over 13,000 homes and buildings. Luckily, only seven people were reported to have died from the fire.

Staying Safe

People, through carelessness, start most fires. By observing a few important rules, fires can be prevented.

Fire codes

Fire codes are a set of rules to help prevent fires, and are regulated by trained fire inspectors. Fire codes state that buildings have smoke detectors installed, floors have two exits, fire extinguishers are located on every floor, and sprinkler systems are installed.

After a fire in a city building or home, fire inspectors determine the cause of the blaze.

Using fire extinguishers

Fire extinguishers are used in small fires. They are important to have installed in kitchens in the home. The word PASS can remind you of the steps for using an extinguisher.

P - Pull the pin
A - Aim the nozzle about ten feet (three meters) from the fire
S - Squeeze the handle
S - Sweep the nozzle from one side of the fire to the other

Be prepared!

- *Together with your family, plan what to do in case of a fire in your home.*

- *Make sure you have two ways out of your bedroom. Before you try to leave your bedroom, check the doorknob. If it feels hot, use a different exit.*

- *Smoke detectors or alarms should be located outside each bedroom and on each level of the home. Carbon monoxide detectors are a good idea on every floor of the house. Test batteries in smoke and carbon monoxide detectors twice a year.*

In case of fire

- *Get down low. Smoke rises up, so crawl along the ground – the air near the floor has more oxygen and is safer to breathe.*

- *If your clothing catches on fire, stop immediately, drop to the ground, cover your face and mouth with your hands, and roll until the fire is out.*

- *Get outside. Once you are outside, do not go back inside.*

- *Call 911*

Fighting Fires

Firefighters are specially trained men and women who bravely risk their lives putting out fires.

At the fire station

In the city, firefighters live in station houses during their shifts. There, they check that equipment and vehicles are in proper working order and set to go in the event of a fire. They also train for fires, do safety courses, and perform household chores.

(top) Emergency calls come from a dispatch center. In city fires, dispatchers give the fire department information. Within 45 seconds, firefighters are on their way to the fire.

(left) This woman is specially trained to fight forest fires.

(opposite page, top) Before arrival, the officer analyzes the fire and its dangers, and decides a fire fighting plan.

Where's the fire?

Each fire engine has a team of firefighters assigned to it - a driver, an officer who directs the firefighters, and the firefighters who put out the fire. On route to the fire, the officer gets information about the location of the fire, and the number of people and types of fuels that are in the building.

Fighting forest fires

Forest rangers take care of natural wildlife areas, and during fire season, fire prevention and control is one of their jobs. Forest fires quickly spread, so forest firefighters from nearby communities join forest rangers in fighting fires.

(below) A central command post is set up to organize the many crews posted at different locations in the forest. They receive weather readings and make decisions on whether firefighters are safe, or need to pull out. They also coordinate rescue teams if firefighters get injured on the job.

Hot Shots

Hot Shots are specially trained forest firefighters who fight the most dangerous wildfires. These firefighters only work during the summer months. When an emergency call comes in they are alerted with beepers, and when they arrive at the scene of a fire, they stay at that location for months, until the fire is controlled. Hot Shot crews work for ten to eighteen hours a day.

Smoke Jumpers

When forest fires cannot be reached by roads, another special group of firefighters are called in: the Smoke Jumpers. They work for up to 16 hours a day to fight fires. Smoke Jumpers are in very good physical shape and carry backpacks that weigh about 85 pounds (39 kg). In the backpacks are flashlights, food, water, portable fire shelters, two-way radios, and other tools for fighting fires. There are only 400 Smoke Jumpers working in the United States.

Smoke Jumpers are flown in by helicopter and parachute into the fire.

These Hot Shots clear a fire line using shovels, rakes, and hoes.

On the job

One method of putting out a forest fire is to remove all the fuel. To do this, a fire line, or fire break, is created. Fire lines are wide areas where firefighters have removed all trees, roots, and debris from the forest floor. Firefighters use hand tools such as axes, hoes, or a pulaski, which has an axe at one end and a hoe at the other, to make a fire line up to ten feet (3.5 meters) wide. Bulldozers are used to build fire lines up to 150 feet (46 meters) wide.

Back-firing is a firefighter's method of fighting fire with fire. Firefighters start a smaller, well-controlled fire well ahead of a larger fire to burn the fuel away. When the larger fire arrives at the already burned area, there will be no fuel left for it to burn, and it will extinguish. This is a dangerous method because it is difficult to keep a back-fire under control. It is only used in extreme situations when fires cannot be stopped and are coming close to residential areas.

Firefighting tools

Two-way radios are for communication between crews and dispatch. City firefighters carry a special tracking device called a Pass, or Pal (Personal Alert Safety System). This device makes a high-pitch noise if the firefighter stops moving. Firefighters carry tools that have an axe-blade at one end, and a poker at the other. The axe is to tear down walls inside a building, and the poker is to check for weak spots in the floor and ceiling. The special clothing firefighters wear is called "turnout gear." Forest firefighters wear helmets and a fire retardant jacket. They carry drip torches for starting back fires, and a pulaski.

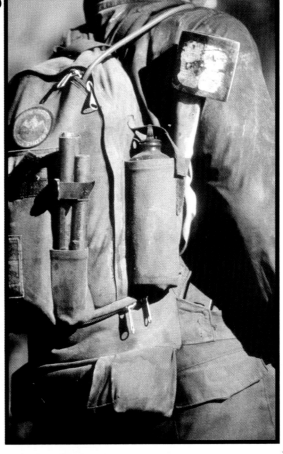

Help from above

When forest fires are too large or dangerous for firefighters on the ground, airplanes and helicopters drop water from a nearby water source. The CL-415 airplane is a water bomber built especially for fighting fires. It has floats and wheels so that it can land on water or air. By skimming over the surface of a lake or river this plane takes in 1,400 gallons (6,000 liters) of water to fill the tanks in its hull in just twelve seconds, and then fly back to the fire. Helicopters can airlift a bucket that holds about 400 gallons (1,500 liters) of water to dump on a fire. The Bell 205 is a helicopter especially designed for fighting fires. It has a tank that holds 300 gallons (1,200 liters) of water, which it draws up through a suction hose that it drops into a water source such as a river or lake.

(below) Fire retardant, or slurry, is a chemical mixed with water to put out fires. The chemicals absorb heat and provide a sticky coating to starve the fire of oxygen. A red dye is added to the retardant so pilots can see where they have already covered.

(above) Water from a nearby lake is dumped on a forest fire.

Adapting to Fires

Although it may look like it, forests do not die after a fire burns through it. Instead, the woodland area is already preparing for new growth.

Trees

A tree's bark is a thick, **insulating** layer that helps protect it from fire. Trees that are alive can be damaged on the outside but their root systems and **inner cores** are still healthy and strong, and the trees will continue to grow.

Cork Oak trees grow in the southern areas of Portugal, Spain, Italy, France, and the northern area of Africa. These trees have bark that is well adapted to drought and forest fires. Cork bark is made up of a very high number of **cells** and contains a waxy substance called suberin, which does not allow liquids or gases to penetrate it. During a fire, the bark insulates the delicate inner tree core, and helps it survive.

The giant sequoia trees on the west coast of North America need forest fires to help the species survive. Sequoia trees have a two foot (60 cm) thick bark that protects them from fire damage.

Fire species

Some species of trees and animals have adapted to fires. These are called fire species. Trees called Lodgepole or Ponderosa pine produce two types of cones. One kind opens during years when there are no fires. The other type of cones, called serotinous cones, are held together by a resin that will only open when heated by flames. When fire burns through a forest of Lodgepole pines most of the trees are killed. The heat from the fire melts the resin and opens the serotinous cones, and releases the seeds to start a new forest of Lodgepole pines.

In southern California, the Chaparral also depends on frequent fires. A flammable resin coats this shrub's leaves, which makes it easy to burn. Also, only the intense heat of fires can crack open the Chaparral's seeds, so a new generation can begin to grow.

Tree rings

Scientists study a forest's fire history by reading the blackened fire scars in a tree's rings. By counting a tree's rings, scientists can also tell how old the tree is. When a fire burns a tree's cambium, the layer of tree just under the bark, it blackens the layer.

(right) The bark of this tree has been badly burned in a forest fire. The tree itself is still alive.

Forest animals

Some animals depend on fire for their existence. In Australia, a species of bird called the firehawk actually starts fires. The birds grab burning twigs, and drop them onto unburned grass to flush out small rodents to hunt. Owls and other predatory birds benefit from the thinning of forest canopies and floors because they can spot their prey easier.

Small animals that live beneath the Earth remain in their burrows until the fire is over. Larger, plant eating animals move to other areas before the fires get near them. Birds fly to safety. When the fire is over, seed-eating animals find a great store of seeds lying on the forest floor. Plant-eating animals return shortly after a fire to find a plentiful and more nutritious food source because of the new plant growth. The nutrients in ash help a number of berry-producing shrubs grow, which in turn draw berry-eating animals such as black bear, deer, and moose to the area. This attracts more predatory animals, such as cougars, to the forest.

(above) This bear cub was rescued from a forest fire.

(below) A bull elk with a singed coat wanders through a newly burned forest.

ELKHART LAKE I M O

Recipe for Disaster

Fire might never happen in your house, but if it does, being prepared and having a family plan could save you and your family's lives. A fire plan is simple and important to do.

What you need:
* pencil   * paper   * red marker   * your family
* smoke detector   * batteries

What to do:

1. Draw a floor plan of your house. If you have two floors - draw both floor plans - include the basement too!

2. In red marker, find two ways out of every room in the house and mark them clearly. Designate a meeting spot outside. When you get outside, stay there until the rest of your family can join you.

3. Check to see that you can open windows for the alternative routes you have marked. Check to see that you can use your escape ladder if your bedroom is on the second floor. Check the fire detector too - it cannot alert you to fire if the batteries are dead.

4. Now it is drill time. Start in your bedroom. Pretend the fire alarm has just gone off. You jump up and feel the door and door handle first. Is it hot? (Your brother shouts that the fire is right outside your door). Run to your alternative exit. If you live on a second floor - this is when you use an escape ladder. Open your window and hang it out and then shout that you are ready to leave.

5. Try it again. This time when the alarm goes off your father shouts that the door and handle are cool. Crouch down and carefully open the door. Head outside to your family meeting place.

6. In the event of a real fire, you would call 911 from your outside meeting place. Calmly tell the dispatcher your name and address. Never go into a house on fire - family pets can take care of themselves, and firefighters will be along shortly to help them if they need it. Do not try to rescue them yourself.

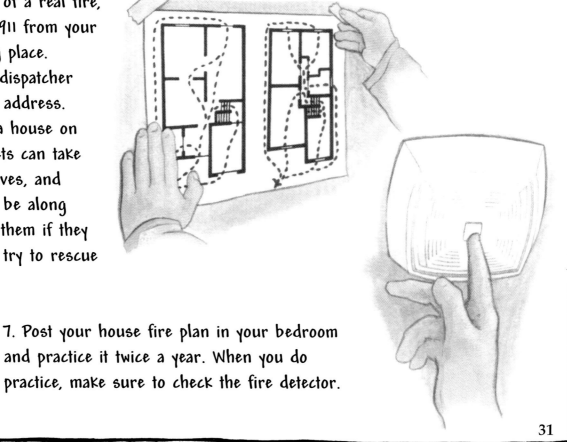

7. Post your house fire plan in your bedroom and practice it twice a year. When you do practice, make sure to check the fire detector.

31

Glossary

ancient Egyptian Belonging to a civilization that lived along the Nile River in Egypt, Africa, from 2850 to 715 B.C.

atmosphere The layers of air and other gases that surround Earth

canopy The top layer of the forest, usually with wide, spreading branches

carbon dioxide A colorless, odorless gas produced when humans breathe

cells The smallest living parts of plants and animals

combustion The development of light and heat from the chemical combination of a substance with oxygen

drought A period of little or no rain

energy Usable power

evaporate To change into a vapor or gas

fertilize To put a substance onto the soil that will make plants grow better

firestorm A large fire that sucks in surrounding wind, making it even more intense

flammable Able to catch fire easily

gas A substance that is neither solid nor liquid

humidity The amount of moisture in the air

inner core The inside wood of a tree

insulate To cover or surround an object with a material that prevents heat from passing through

intense Very strong

minerals Non-living substances created by nature

organic Living, or used to be living

precipitation Water that falls to Earth in the form of rain and snow

sapling A very young tree

suppress To hold back or put an end to

volatile An object that has parts that can evaporate quickly

Index

1 2 3 4 5 6 7 8 9 0 Printed in the U.S.A. 3 2 1 0 9 8 7 6 5 4